Gangs and the Abuse of Power

TOOKIE SPEAKS OUT AGAINST GANG VIOLENCE™

Stanley "Tookie" Williams

with Barbara Cottman Becnel

The Rosen Publishing Group's
PowerKids Press™
New York

Published in 1996 by The Rosen Publishing Group, Inc.
29 East 21st Street, New York, NY 10010

First Edition

Book design: Kim Sonsky

Photo credits: Cover © Wilson North/International Stock; front cover inset, back cover and p. 4 © J. Patrick Forden; p. 7 by Kim Sonsky; p. 8 © Skjold; p. 11 © Roger Markham Smith/International Stock; pp. 12, 19 © Scott Thode/International Stock; p. 15 © Bill Stanton/International Stock; pp. 16, 20 by Michael Brandt.

Williams, Stanley.
    Gangs and the abuse of power / Stanley "Tookie" Williams, with Barbara Cottman Becnel.
       p.   cm. — (Tookie speaks out against gang violence)
    Includes index.
    Summary: The co-founder of the Crips tells how gang members abuse the power they have to hurt others and ultimately hurt themselves.
    ISBN 0-8239-2346-0
    1. Gangs—United States—Juvenile literature. 2. Juvenile delinquency—United States—Juvenile literature. 3. Dominance (Psychology)—United States—Juvenile literature. [1. Gangs. 2. Dominance (Psychology).] I. Becnel, Barbara Cottman. II. Title. III. Series: Williams, Stanley. Tookie speaks out against gang violence.
HV6439.U5W565 1996
364.1'06'60973—dc20   96-6087
                                                  CIP
                                                  AC

Manufactured in the United States of America

Contents

Walking in the 'Hood

When I was a teenager, I liked walking the streets of my South Central Los Angeles **'hood** (HOOD). And so did my **homeboys** (HOME-boyz). Sometimes there were so many of us that we blocked the sidewalk. No one could get by.

One day about seventy of us walked past my uncle's house. He saw me in the crowd and yelled my nickname, "Tookie!" Later my uncle told me, "Until I saw it was you with those boys, I was scared." I liked that. Grown-ups were afraid of us.

◀ *Tookie learned that it is easy to abuse power.*
Now he teaches people to respect each other.

Power

    For my homeboys and me, **power** (POW-er) meant other people were so scared of us they would do whatever we wanted. We would make them give us their money, jewelry, or leather coats. We **abused** (uh-BYOUZD) the power we had over people. Many gang members abuse their power. I've learned that nothing good ever comes from abusing power to scare or hurt people.

Some people use their power to scare or hurt other people. ▶

Protecting Ourselves

When I was 17, I met Raymond Washington, who hung out with a lot of homeboys from the east side of South Central. My homeboys and I were from the west side. Raymond and I decided that we would have even more power if we got our homeboys together. We created a gang called the Crips.

At first, we used our power only to protect ourselves, our families, and friends from other gangs. But then hundreds of kids joined the Crips. We saw that we could use our power to get whatever we wanted. So we did.

◀ *Many gangs abuse the power that they have.*

"Crips Don't Die"

As the Crips grew from hundreds to thousands of members, we felt that we had so much power we couldn't get hurt. We thought we were real tough. We started saying, "Crips don't die, we **multiply**" (MUL-ti-ply). And back then, we believed it.

But soon we had to face the sad truth. Crips could die. The more we hurt other people, the more they hurt us back. Crips were getting killed. But that didn't stop us from abusing our power.

Many kids don't believe that they can be hurt or even killed. ▶

Mobbing

We learned that if we walked around the 'hood in big crowds, we could usually get anything we wanted. If forty of us stepped onto a bus, we didn't have to pay. The bus driver was too afraid to ask for our fares. People called what we did **mobbing** (MOB-bing).

We mobbed our way into concerts, movie theaters, and stores. We never paid for anything. We didn't stop to think about right or wrong. That's why we got into so much trouble.

◄ *There is strength in numbers. But that strength must be used for the right reasons.*

Gangbanging

Sometimes mobbing wasn't enough. Then we used fear and violence to get people to do what we wanted. We called that **gangbanging** (GANG-bang-ing). We also began to use more than just our fists. We used weapons.

Soon we were gangbanging more than mobbing. Someone always got hurt.

Weapons cause more and more people to get hurt. ▶

Gang Members Are Afraid Too

Even though gang members use their power to scare other people, many gang members are scared too. Some gangbang because they are afraid of losing their friends if they don't. Some act tough to hide their fear of hurting other people, or of getting hurt. But mostly kids are afraid of letting other gang members know how scared they are. So they keep quiet and keep scaring and hurting others.

◀ *Most kids are afraid to let others know that they are scared of hurting others or being hurt. They act tough to hide their fear.*

Abusing Power

As a teenager, I didn't know the meaning of power. I thought that by using violence to scare people, I was proving that I had a lot of power. But when you use your power to make someone do something they don't want to do, or to hurt someone, you are abusing your power.

The people you hurt will some day hurt you. They may call your parents to tell them the bad things you've done. They may call the police and have you arrested. They may even use a weapon on you.

People who hurt others run the risk of being arrested by the police. ▶

Sometimes Less Is Better

I grew up poor and wanted a lot of things that other kids had. Most of my homeboys were poor too. We would gangbang to get what our parents couldn't afford to buy us.

But now I know it's better to have less of the things you want than to get them by stealing, selling drugs, or hurting others. You create **enemies** (EN-em-ees) when you abuse power. In prison, I don't own very much. But I don't hurt or frighten anyone to get what I have. And that feels good.

◄ *Feeling good about yourself and the way you treat others are the best things you can do.*

The Power Within You

Real power is already inside each one of us. Real power is having power over yourself, not over other people. Joining a gang, using weapons, mobbing, or gang-banging won't give you real power. You get real power over your life by making good choices every day about what you do and who you hang out with. If you don't belong to a gang, use the power within you to stay away from them. If you are a member of a gang, use the power within you to walk away. I did it, so I know you can do it too.

Glossary

abuse (uh-BYOUZ) Use in a bad way.

enemy (EN-em-ee) Someone who wants to hurt you.

gangbanging (GANG-bang-ing) Gang members using violence against other people or to commit crimes.

homeboy (HOME-boy) Friend or partner.

'hood (HOOD) Slang word for neighborhood.

mobbing (MOB-bing) Large number of kids pushing to get what they want.

multiply (MUL-ti-ply) Growing in number.

power (POW-er) Strength; control over yourself or others.

Index